NOAH
AND
THE VERY FIRST RAINBOW
by Sunny Griffin

Illustrated by Donna Lee

DID YOU KNOW...
God was unhappy
with all the bad
people on the earth?

DID YOU KNOW...
Noah was the
only good man
He could find?

DID YOU KNOW...
God told Noah
to build a big boat
called an ark?

DID YOU KNOW...

The bad people all laughed at Noah as he built the ark?

DID YOU KNOW...
God told Noah
to put all kinds
of animals and
birds on the ark?

DID YOU KNOW...
After Noah and
his family got on
the ark, God closed
the big door?

DID YOU KNOW...
Water covered the earth for a long, long time?

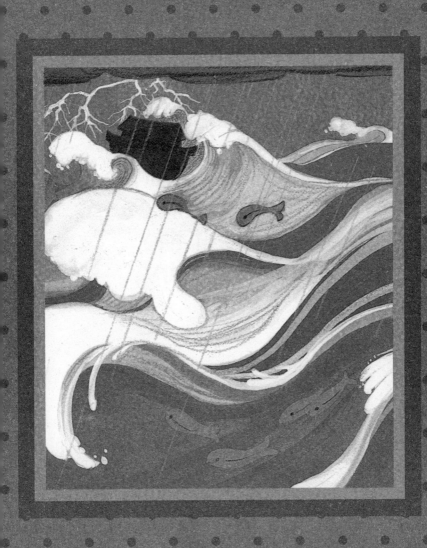

DID YOU KNOW...
Noah sent a dove
out three times
to see if the
land was dry?

DID YOU KNOW...

After the water went away, Noah and the animals got off the ark?

DID YOU KNOW...
Noah and his family thanked God for keeping them safe and dry?

DID YOU KNOW...
God was happy
with Noah for
obeying Him?

DID YOU KNOW...
God put the very first rainbow in the sky for Noah?

A rainbow is God's promise He will never cover the earth with water again.